THE COMPLETE BOOK OF SPIDER-MAN: INTO THE SPIDER-VERSE
A CENTUM BOOK 978-1-912707-29-4
Published in Great Britain by Centum Books Ltd
This edition published 2018
1 3 5 7 9 10 8 6 4 2

© 2018 MARVEL © 2018 SPA & CPII

Centum Books Ltd, 20 Devon Square, Newton Abbot, Devon, TQ12 2HR, UK

books@centumbooksltd.co.uk

CENTUM BOOKS Limited Reg. No. 07641486

A CIP catalogue record for this book is available from the British Library

Printed in Italy.

The Complete Book of SPIDER-MAN

INTO THE SPIDER-VERSE

This web-tastic book belongs to:

centum

Contents

See answers on pages 60-61.

Swing into the Spider-Verse!

Follow the journey of Miles Morales, as he goes from being an ordinary 13-year-old Brooklyn boy to becoming the new Spider-Man. Meet all the members of Miles' Spidey family including his mentor, the original Spider-Man, Peter Parker.

Read an exciting Spidey story, check out the super-cool character profiles and complete web-loads of puzzles and activities.

Ultimate bad guy, the Kingpin, and his team of thugs are hiding throughout this book. Tick off the Super Villains as you spot them on the pages.

Ready, set, SWING!

Page:

Page:

Page:

Tombstone

Green Goblin

Kingpin

Page:

Scorpion

Page:

Prowler

Profiles

Meet The Family

Each member of the Spidey family is from a different world within the Spider-Verse, but they've been brought together to help the new Spider-Man, Miles. Read all about them here!

Quote:

"You need to learn about maintaining control of your abilities."

Gwen

Name: Gwen Stacy

Spidey name: Spider-Gwen

Age: 15

Bitten by: Radioactive spider

Costume colours: Black, white, pink and turquoise

Powers: Wall-crawling, web-spinning, web-swinging

Weapons: Web-shooters

Can be: Sharp

Peni

Name: Peni Parker

Spidey name: SP//dr

Age: 13

Lives: Tokyo

Family: Father

World: Earth #3932

Bitten by: Radioactive spider

Costume colours: Red, blue and black

Peni's powers: None

SP//dr's powers: Wall-crawling, web-spinning, web-swinging

Weapons: SP//dr robot-suit, web-shooters

Can be: Sarcastic

Quote:

"Let me tell you a thing or thirty about electrical engineering..."

10

Porker

Name: Peter Porker
Spidey name: Spider-Ham
World: Earth #584
Bitten by: Radioactive pig
Species then: Spider
Species now: Pig
Costume colours: Red and blue
Powers: Wall-crawling, web-spinning, web-swinging
Weapons: Web-shooters
Can be: A bit of a joker

Quote:

"Disinfect the mask. Trust me. I'm a pig."

Noir

Name: Peter Parker
Spidey name: Spider-Man Noir
World: Earth #1938
Bitten by: Non-radioactive spider
Costume colours: Black
Powers: Wall-crawling, web-spinning, web-swinging
Weapons: Web-shooters
Can be: Very serious

Quote:

"Punch, punch, kick, punch, head fake, head fake, head fake..."

SUPER HERO SCHOOLBOY

Read all about how Miles Morales went from ordinary schoolboy to awesome Super Hero overnight. He soon discovers that having Spidey skills isn't always easy — in fact, it can lead to some totally embarrassing situations!

IT'S TIME FOR A SPIDER-MAN ADVENTURE...

1.

Miles Morales sings along to the tunes blaring through his headphones as he rushes around his bedroom, packing for Brooklyn Visions Academy.

5. *I've got this*, Miles repeats to himself as he enters school. Miles nods and smiles at his peers as he walks through the hallways, refusing to be deterred when no one smiles back.

6. But the day gets worse as it goes along: packed schedules, endless instructions, and most of all – mountains of homework.

BLAH

BLAH

BLAH

BLAH

BLAH

BLAH

BLAH

HOW AM I EVER GOING TO MANAGE?

BLAH

BLAH

BLAH

BLAH

American History

7. Later that evening, Miles sits in his dorm facing piles of work. His roommate, Ganke, is reading. Ganke and Miles aren't quite friends yet. Miles sighs, lonely and bored. His phone chimes and he smiles, looking at the text message. This is just what he needs to cheer him up.

8. A LITTLE WHILE LATER, MILES IS CLIMBING UP HIS UNCLE AARON'S FIRE ESCAPE.

Hey Miles! What's up? Wanna come over?

HI, UNCLE AARON!

HEY, MILES!

I HAVE A SURPRISE FOR YOU, NEPHEW!

Continued on page 32. **15**

Spidey Spinner

How to play:

Cut out the spinner below and stick it onto card. Once it's dry, push a pencil through the middle. Each morning, twirl the pencil to spin the spinner. Whichever Spidey rests on the table when it stops is the Spidey you will be for the day!

Ask an adult to help you cut out your spinner. Finish the story on page 43 first!

Pretend to be a Spidey every day and use your spinner to pick which one. Talk the talk and crawl the crawl!

WWSSHH!!!

SPIDER-MAN

"KID" ARACHNID

SPIDER-HAM

SPYDR & PENI PARKER

SPIDER-MAN NOIR

SPIDER-GWEN

Here's some info on each Spidey, to help you play the part...

Miles Morales
- bright, funny, enthusiastic, confident

Peter Parker
- positive, patient, a good teacher

Gwen Stacy
- intelligent, a natural leader, quick-witted, sharp sense of humour

Spider-Man Noir
- serious, old-fashioned, lacks a sense of humour

Peni Parker
- throws tantrums, loves all things tech, very expressive

Peter Porker
- sweet, kind, pays a lot of compliments, cracks a lot of jokes

WHO IS MILES MORALES?

THE NEW SPIDER-MAN

THE END!

Double Puzzle

Miles is using the cover of darkness to test out his new Spidey skills. Can you complete the two black-and-white puzzles?

Which piece doesn't belong to either picture?

52

Teams Of Two

miles

Peni

Peter

noir

Gwen

Ham

53

Gwen's Grid

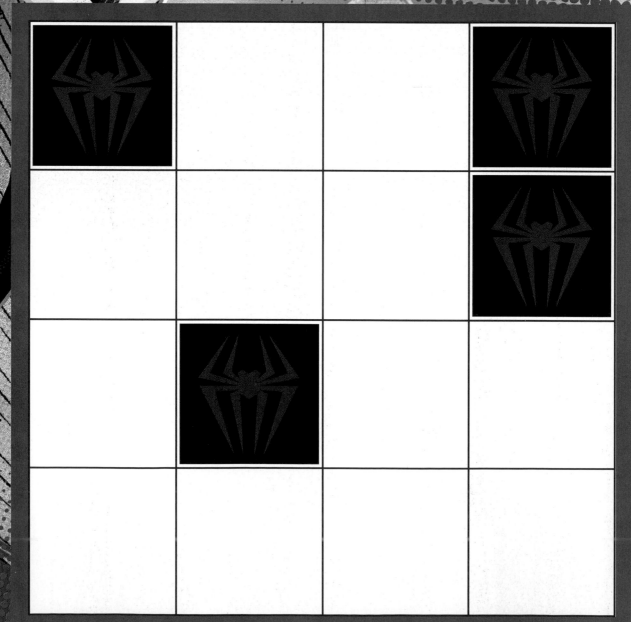

54

SP//dr

SPIDER-MAN
INTO THE SPIDER-VERSE

永遠に
メタル

Answers

Page 7

Kingpin – page 17

Prowler – page 25

Scorpion – page 30

Green Goblin – page 42

Tombstone – page 47

Pages 16-17

L	I	E	U	P	A	E	L	D	S	W	I	A	C	C
F	R	J	A	M	O	C	J	D	G	S	U	P	E	R
P	E	A	T	V	N	W	O	L	X	T	D	V	O	O
Y	S	Y	D	X	S	N	E	U	X	R	V	P	Z	U
K	P	T	T	I	F	C	E	R	K	E	N	A	T	C
T	O	Z	S	Y	O	R	M	D	T	T	F	P	T	H
A	N	D	Z	V	U	A	I	J	O	C	I	S	E	O
M	S	E	Q	P	T	W	C	J	Z	H	W	Y	H	M
K	I	W	J	X	T	L	Y	T	Y	L	C	W	E	B
M	B	G	I	C	W	S	X	F	I	U	Q	U	R	L
N	I	O	J	N	T	G	E	D	Q	V	K	N	O	G
L	L	T	S	V	G	L	S	P	I	D	E	R	P	X
N	I	P	S	S	A	K	M	V	P	I	O	O	S	P
A	T	M	I	G	L	U	O	P	L	G	A	L	S	M
O	Y	P	Q	M	J	V	S	E	I	G	P	L	K	A

Page 18

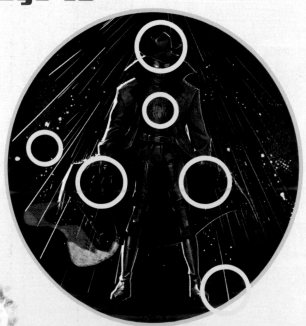

Page 28

1. False   2. True   3. False   4. False
5. True   6. False   7. True

Page 29

Peter's webbing is the longest.

Page 30

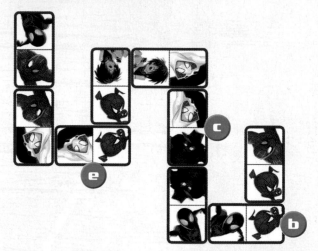

Page 31

Spin – 4
Web – 3

Page 38

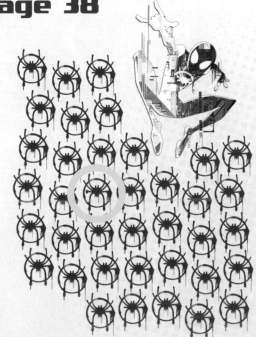

Page 41

The number to dial is: 2 9 5 2 7 8 3 1 4 6.

Pages 42-43

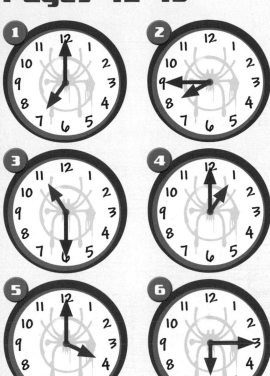

Page 45

a – f   b – k   c – h
d – g   e – j   i – l

Page 46-47

Page 52

Piece d doesn't belong to either picture.

Page 53

Miles – Ham

Peni – Noir

Peter – Gwen

Page 54

	2	2	3	3
3	■	□	■	■
1	□	□	□	■
4	■	■	■	■
2	□	■	■	□

Page 59

S	S	A	D	S	A	P	E	P	M
P	M	S	I	E	I	S	S	S	E
S	D	S	P	M	S	E	A	I	S
A	D	S	N	E	S	A	S	I	S
N	S	M	P	S	A	I	D	N	S
S	I	N	S	D	M	E	S	S	D
S	P	I	S	I	M	S	P	N	P
P	S	S	P	D	S	N	N	S	M
M	D	A	E	M	S	E	S	D	S
S	M	D	S	E	I	S	P	I	S

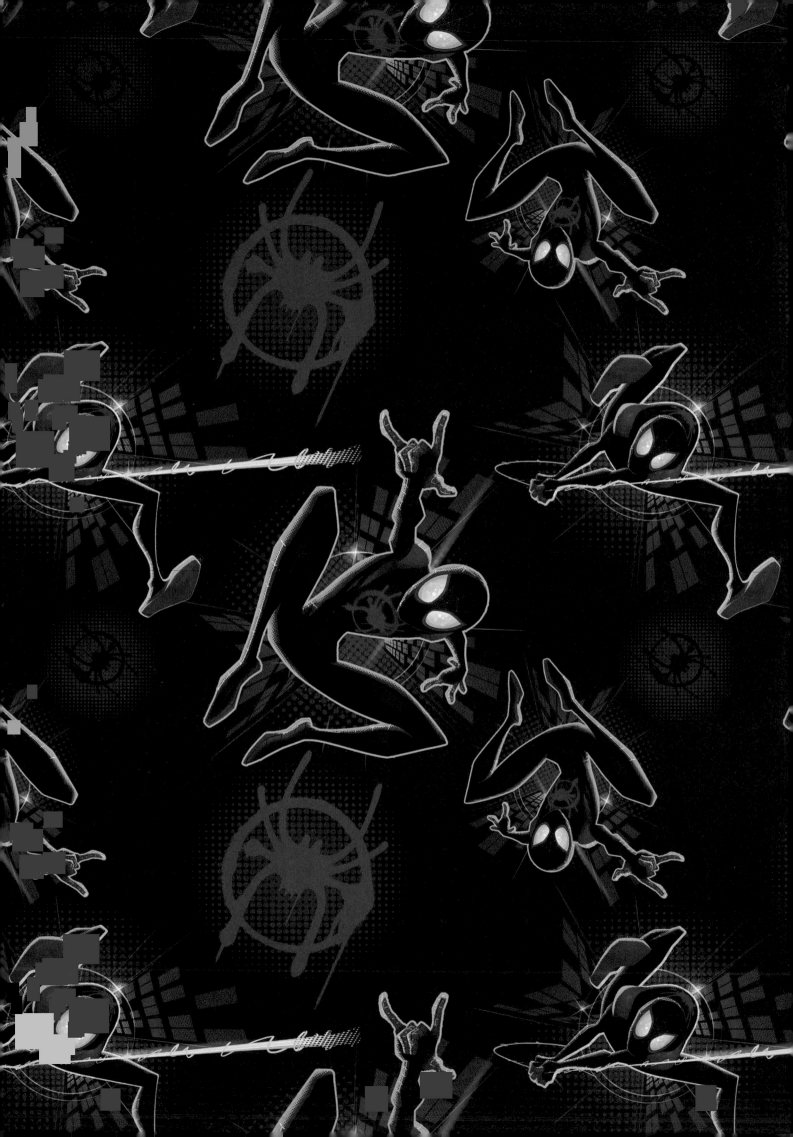